The Runaway Day

Written & illustrated by
LeeAnn Rost

Interior Image Credit: LeeAnn Rost

WestBow Press books may be ordered through booksellers or by contacting:

WestBow Press
A Division of Thomas Nelson & Zondervan
1663 Liberty Drive
Bloomington, IN 47403
www.westbowpress.com
1 (866) 928-1240

ISBN: 978-1-9736-6240-2 (sc)
ISBN: 978-1-9736-6241-9 (e)

Library of Congress Control Number: 2019907126

Print information available on the last page.

WestBow Press rev. date: 06/14/2019

WESTBOW
PRESS®
A DIVISION OF THOMAS NELSON
& ZONDERVAN

LeeAnn's first book, The Runaway Day, is a compilation of her happy childhood memories and an important lesson she learned. Now a grandmother, she still loves spending time with children and wants to help parents convey Godly principles to their children. Her six children, now all grown, gave her many ideas, so watch for more of her delightful stories!

Dedicated to Nathan, Slater,
JJ, Elizabeth, Everett, Owen,
and my yet unborn grandchildren,
who are all my sunshines.

It was a warm, sunshiny day on that day we ran away, my big brother, my sister and me.

We tried to be good and to behave, my brother, my sister and me. But sometimes we were having so much fun that we forgot, especially on warm, sunshiny days.

We'd been warned and we'd been told. Playing in my daddy's wagon was bad and would make him mad. But we did it anyway, my brother, my sister and me. The wagon was big and gray with two black wheels under the middle. We ran to the top end that was high in the air and waited for it to crash to the ground...CA-BUMP! Then we turned around and raced to the other end and again...CA-BUMP! We were mighty munchkins balancing on a titanic teeter totter!

CA-BOOM!!

LeeAnn Rost

Then daddy saw us, and he WAS mad. Once again he told us that we couldn't play in his big gray wagon, my brother, my sister or me. He said it wasn't a teeter totter and that we might break it. WE didn't think we would break daddy's wagon on that warm, sunshiny day.

We'd been warned and we'd been told. Playing on the roof of my daddy's tool shed was bad and would make him mad, but we did it anyway, my brother, my sister and me. My brother found a ladder and we climbed up on it. Up onto the roof we went. We were mighty mountain climbers on a purple, mammoth mountain!

Then daddy saw us and he WAS mad.
Once again he told us that we couldn't play
on the roof of his tool shed, my brother, my
sister or me. He said it wasn't a mountain and
we might fall off and get hurt. WE didn't think
that we would fall off and get hurt on that
warm, sunshiny day.

We'd been warned and we'd been told. Playing with grapes was bad and would make daddy mad, but we did it anyway, my brother, my sister and me. We stuffed the purple grapes into our mouths till they could hold no more, the sticky juice dripping down our tanned faces. Then in front of my baby blue eyes I spied the biggest grape I'd ever seen. My mouth being full, what else could I do? I plucked it off the leafy vine and flung it straight at my brother's face. It splatted on his forehead, wet and sticky. He shot one back. Then my sister joined in with glee. Soon grapes were flying everywhere around us all three. We were great "grape warriors" fighting for our lives!

Then daddy saw us and he WAS mad. Once again he told us that we couldn't play with the grapes. He said that we weren't "grape warriors" and that we might hurt someone in the eye on that warm, sunshiny day.

We'd been warned and we'd been told. Playing in the mud was bad and would make daddy mad, but we did it anyway, my brother, my sister and me. We found a ditch full of mud from yesterday's rain, all wet and sloppy, and oh, so inviting! We stood at the top of the ditch trying to decide what to do. Then, with a giggle, I took the plunge and landed…KER-SPLISH! One glance at my brother's grinning face and I knew he would be next…KER-SPLASH! Then my sister took the plunge…KER-SPLISH! We were portly pigs pluckily playing in our pigpen!

Then daddy saw us and he WAS mad. Once again he told us that we couldn't play in the mud, my brother, my sister or me. He said that we weren't "portly pigs" and that we could ruin our bright summer clothes. WE didn't think we could ruin our clothes on that bright, sunshiny day.

WE decided that we'd had enough of 'couldn'ts' and 'don'ts' on that warm, sunshiny day. Yes, we'd been warned and we'd been told. Running away was dangerous and we could get hungry or cold. But we'd had enough and so that was that, the decision was made. My brother brought his slingshot in case we saw a bear. My sister took some sticky buns and said that she would share. Above us was the warm sun; what was there to fear? So down the dusty, country road we walked. We walked quite a ways, my brother, my sister and me.

We prattled along playfully as we pranced down the road on that warm, sunshiny day. But soon the sun started to sink and we started to shiver and shake. Then we were starved and each ate a sticky bun. But our stomachs still grumbled and growled for some more as we walked on in the scary darkening dusk. In our misery we no longer felt so bold. Why didn't we listen to our daddy when he said that we shouldn't run away, my brother, my sister or me?

Frozen with fear is what we were next as we peered at the frightening form in the hollowed old oak, on that dark, runaway day. Its eyes were aglow. Its teeth white as snow. As we stood staring, our stomachs still squawking, suddenly, with a fright, we all came to know that brother's slingshot would be useless against such a fiendish foe. Oh, why didn't we listen to our dear daddy when he said that it might be dangerous to run away, my brother, my sister or me?

Then with a start, we heard a rumble and roar. We turned to see a car creeping slowly down the road towards us, on that dark, runaway day. We'd heard about strangers who sometimes might steal you and we leaped into the deep grass of the ditch. Stomachs still growling, shrinking and squawking, monsters in trees; teeth white as snow, strangers who sometimes might steal you. We thought of all this as we lie in the ditch shivering and shaking. Why, oh why didn't we listen to our dear daddy, my brother, my sister, or me?

A sudden loud wail and a thud right beside us was all that it took to cause us to yell, on that dark, runaway day. "HELP!" we all cried out at once. Then the rumbling of the old car came to a stop at the top of the ditch. The stranger must have heard us! Now he might steal us and take us away! If only we'd listened to our dear daddy and all of the things that he'd told us and taught us, we might not be hungry, or frightened or cold, my brother, my sister, or me.

A dark form loomed above us as we lay in the ditch, my brother, my sister and me. We fearfully opened our eyes and peeked up. Much to our happy, hilarious glee, what did we see on that dark, runaway day? It was our own dear daddy! We all ran to hug him, forgetting that he probably was mad. But Daddy said that he was happy we were all safe and sound, that the danger was done and we could all drive home. Drive home we did to warm food and beds and a big hug from mom who had been filled with such dread.

Our punishment was dusting and polishing all week, but we didn't mind so very much. We had learned that parents know best after all. We knew we were loved, THAT we could see. And so, after that, we tried very much harder to mind and behave, my brother, my sister and me.

"Children, obey your parents in
the Lord, for this is right."
Ephesians 6:1

Printed in the United States
By Bookmasters